CONTEMPORARY LIVES

GRAMMY-WINNING SUPERSTAR

ABDO
Publishing Company

CONTEMPORARY LIVES

RIHANNA

GRAMMY-WINNING SUPERSTAR

by DeAnn Herringshaw

CREDITS

Published by ABDO Publishing Company, PO Box 398166, Minneapolis,
MN 55439. Copyright © 2014 by Abdo Consulting Group, Inc. International
copyrights reserved in all countries. No part of this book may be reproduced
in any form without written permission from the publisher. The Essential
Library™ is a trademark and logo of ABDO Publishing Company.

Printed in the United States of America,
North Mankato, Minnesota
082013
012014

Editor: Megan Anderson
Series Designer: Emily Love

Photo credits: Shutterstock Images, cover, 3, 15, 19, 46, 93,
97 (bottom); Matt Sayles/AP Images, 6, 9, 76, 78; Adam J. Sablich/
Shutterstock Images, 16; Tammie Arroyo/AP Images, 23; Rob Verhorst/
Redferns/Getty Images, 26; Jody Cortes/WENN Photos/Newscom, 30; Jason
DeCrow/AP Images, 33, 42, 97 (top); Jeff Christensen/AP Images, 36; Obed
Zilwa/AP Images, 44; Kevork Djansezian/AP Images, 50, 96; Mark J. Terril/
AP Images, 54, 98; Steve Jennings/WireImage/Getty Images, 57; Dimitrios
Kambouris/WireImage/Getty Images, 58; Lester Cohen/WireImage/Getty
Images, 61; Jackson Lee/starmaxinc.com/Newscom, 66, 99 (top); AP Images,
68; Joe Seer/Shutterstock Images, 71; Universal Studios/Photofest, 75; Rex
Features/AP Images, 82; Catchlight Media/Featureflash/Shutterstock Images,
85; Arthur Mola/Invision/AP Images, 86, 99 (bottom); John Shearer/Invision/
AP Images, 90; Jon Furniss/Invision/AP Images, 95

Library of Congress Control Number: 2013946064

Cataloging-in-Publication Data

Herringshaw, DeAnn.
 Rihanna: Grammy-winning superstar / DeAnn Herringshaw.
  p. cm. -- (Contemporary lives)
Includes bibliographical references and index.
ISBN 978-1-62403-227-1
1. Rihanna, 1988- --Juvenile literature. 2. Singers--Biography--Juvenile
literature.   1. Title.
782.42164092--dc23
[B]

2013946064

CONTENTS

1 · **THE POWER OF RIHANNA** 6

2 **ISLAND GIRL** 16

3 **RISING STAR** 26

4 **FLYING AS RIHANNA** 36

5 ***GOOD GIRL GONE BAD*** 46

6 **DISTURBING EVENTS** 58

7 ***LOUD* AND PROUD** 68

8 **LIFE IN THE SPOTLIGHT** 78

9 **THE FUTURE OF RIHANNA** 86

TIMELINE 96

GET THE SCOOP 100

GLOSSARY 102

ADDITIONAL RESOURCES 104

SOURCE NOTES 106

INDEX 110

ABOUT THE AUTHOR 112

Rihanna is known for her electric and sometimes provocative performances.

The Power of Rihanna

||||||||||||||||||||||||||||||||||||||||||||||||||||||||||||||||

On November 23, 2008, Rihanna stood on a glass and steel scaffold towering above the Nokia Theatre L.A. Live stage at the American Music Awards (AMAs) in Los Angeles, California. She wore a tight black outfit with long silver tassels, high-heeled black boots, elbow-length black gloves, and a diamond-studded eye patch. Then the announcer said, "She has more Number 1 hits in this decade than any other female artist. Please welcome Rihanna!"[1]

Rihanna launched into her hit song "Rehab," while gliding along the scaffold. Then she removed the eye patch and came down to the main stage. Amid red lights, pink smoke, and orange flames, she finished the song in front of a cheering crowd.

But performing "Rehab" wasn't the only time the hip-hop and rhythm and blues (R&B) artist illuminated the awards show. Rihanna came onstage again to accept two awards. She won the AMA for Favorite Soul/R&B Female Artist, after she was nominated alongside singers Alicia Keys and Mary J. Blige. She won the same award in 2007, so her 2008 win made her the first female since 1979 to win in consecutive years. Rihanna also went on

R&B GREATS

The first woman to win the American Music Award for Favorite Soul/R&B Female Artist two years in a row was singer Aretha Franklin in 1976 and 1977. Singer Natalie Cole won the same award in 1978 and 1979.

Both Franklin and Cole have played important roles in the evolution of modern music. They have also influenced current female artists, such as Mariah Carey, Alicia Keys, Beyoncé Knowles, and many more.

In 2008, Rihanna became the first since 1979 to win the AMA for Favorite Soul/R&B Female Artist two years in a row.

to win Favorite Pop/Rock Female Artist, beating out Keys and singer Mariah Carey.

In both acceptance speeches, Rihanna was thankful but cool and calm—almost dismissive, a characteristic often associated with the singer. Even though she said winning was "a big deal," because the awards were very prestigious, she acted as if it wasn't a big deal at all.[2] Earlier in 2008, she had

The 2008 Grammy Awards were a big deal for Rihanna. She was obviously thrilled when she won the Best Rap/Sung Collaboration award for the song "Umbrella," featuring rapper Jay Z. Before going onstage, she gave Jay Z a hug and insisted he accompany her. She acknowledged her father, Ronald, saying, "Dad, I know I promised you I'm going to give you my first Grammy, but we're going to have to fight for this one!"[3] With her win, Rihanna also became the first Barbadian to win a Grammy. She held up her new Grammy trophy and gave a shout-out to her homeland: "Barbados! We got one!"[4]

Jay Z teased Rihanna by interrupting and pretending to translate, acting as if the audience couldn't understand her slight accent. After a second interruption, Rihanna jokingly shushed the rapper. She concluded her speech by thanking her family and everyone involved in making the song. Before leaving the stage, Rihanna playfully punched Jay Z, calling him "silly."[5]

won a Grammy Award for her hit song "Umbrella," six Barbados Music Awards, and seven *Billboard* Music Awards, among others. For the young superstar, it seemed as though winning the biggest awards in the music industry was becoming a routine.

||||||||||||||||||||||||||||||||||||||||||||||||||||||||

SUPERSTAR POWER

Rihanna has become one of the most successful recording artists in the world. She has won six AMAs, 19 *Billboard* Music Awards, seven Grammy Awards, multiple Barbados Music Awards, five Black Entertainment Television (BET) Awards, and many more. In 2011, at age 23, Rihanna broke the record for the youngest artist to have 11 songs reach Number 1 on the *Billboard* Hot 100 music chart. She also broke singer Madonna's record of reaching 20 singles on *Billboard*'s Top 10 faster than any other individual artist.

In 2012, *Forbes* ranked her as one of the top five most powerful celebrities, with an income of $53 million during the year. Also in 2012, *Time* magazine called Rihanna "one of the coolest, hottest, most talented, most liked, most listened

BILLBOARD RECORD

On April 22, 2013, Rihanna set a new record for the most Number 1 hits on the *Billboard* Pop Songs radio airplay chart record with ten. Just before she set the record, Rihanna was tied with her good friend and fellow singer Katy Perry at nine Number 1 radio hits each. Rihanna tweeted the announcement with a link to the *Billboard* article, saying: "It's a big day in *Billboard* history!!!! We Rihwrite records over here!"[6]

to, most followed, most impressive artists at work today . . . . She gives . . . not just herself but her energy and spirit."[7]

In the world of social media, Rihanna has also been very influential. As of June 2013, her Facebook page had racked up approximately 72 million fans, more than any other fan page in the world—including pages for popular artists such as Eminem, Lady Gaga, and Shakira. More than 30 million people followed her Twitter account, @rihanna, making her the third most followed Twitter user in the world as of June 2013. Many of the tweets and photos posted on her Instagram account, badgalriri, have turned into tabloid and magazine headlines. Through her use of social media, Rihanna has been very open about things such as her love life, party antics, and the

FAN BASE

The most devoted members of Rihanna's fan base refer to themselves as "RihannaNavy." They typically interact with each other on Facebook and Twitter. Other popular artists have also had fun names for their fan bases. "Lil Waniacs" are fans of rapper Lil Wayne, "KatyCats" are Katy Perry fans, and "Little Monsters" are Lady Gaga fans. Devout fans of singer Justin Bieber are frequently referred to as "Beliebers."

latest targets of her admiration or her anger. Most days there is a story in the media about Rihanna picked up from her activities on Facebook, Twitter, and Instagram.

|||||||||||||||||||||||||||||||||||||||||||||||||||||||||||

HARD WORK AND COLLABORATIONS

Rihanna has been called "a workhorse" and is known for pushing herself and being very productive.[8] By November 2012, she had released seven albums in seven years, a rare achievement for a pop star, and toured all over the world. She is considered "a 24/7 music fixture . . . and one of pop's most broad-minded artists," because she is constantly adding new genres of music to her repertoire and making each song her own.[9] Rihanna's musical style has incorporated Caribbean music, reggae, pop, R&B, hip-hop, dancehall, dance-pop, and rock and roll.

Rihanna is not only a singer but also a songwriter and collaborator. She has worked with talented artists such as Jay Z, Eminem, Drake, and Justin Timberlake. Her voice has appeared on the albums of other musicians, and she also features other artists on her albums. Collaborating with respected artists is not only fun, it has broadened her fan base and helped capture attention for other artists. The ability to work well with others has been very advantageous for Rihanna.

Since she burst onto the music scene in 2005, Rihanna seemingly has had it all: breathtaking beauty, a lovely singing voice, and a dazzling stage presence. But Rihanna's life hasn't been easy. Like so many of her fans, she knows what it is like to feel anxious, lonely, and abused. She has used this pain in creative ways to become a strong and independent female singer. Rihanna has certainly come a long way from her roots in Barbados, the tropical island in the Caribbean, where she was born.

||||||||||

Rihanna has become a popular, at times controversial, singer since she launched her career in 2005.

Growing up in Barbados, Robyn used music as an escape from her troubled home life.

CHAPTER 2

Island Girl

|||||||||||||||||||||||||||||||||||||||||||||||||||||||||||||

Robyn Rihanna Fenty was born on February 20, 1988, in Saint Michael Parish, Barbados, an island in the southeastern portion of the Caribbean Sea. Her mother, Monica Braithwaite, originally from Guyana in northern South America, worked as an accountant. Her father, Ronald Fenty, was a native of Barbados and worked as a warehouse supervisor at a clothing factory. When Robyn was two years old, her brother Rorrey was born.

Robyn's family moved from Saint Michael to Bridgetown when she was very young. They lived in a tiny house in a humble neighborhood, where she attended elementary school at Charles F. Broome Memorial Primary School. When she was ten years old, her youngest brother, Rajad, was born.

BARBADOS

Barbados is a triangular island measuring approximately 20 miles (32 km) at its longest point and 15 miles (24 km) east to west at its widest point. The city of Bridgetown is its capital and main seaport, and more than one-third of the island's population lives in Bridgetown.

The British colonized Barbados in the early 1600s. Plantation owners brought thousands of enslaved people from West Africa to labor in the mills, homes, and sugarcane fields. The white plantation owners grew wealthy and led lives of ease, while slaves were oppressed.

Slavery in Barbados was abolished in 1834. At the time, there were 88,000 blacks and mixed race people but only approximately 15,000 whites. Whites still held most of the political and social power, creating inequality. Most people of black or mixed race descent lived in poverty.

Barbados became independent from the United Kingdom in 1966, and the country has been building a strong national identity by fostering cultural pride in its African heritage. People from Barbados are called Barbadian or Bajan.

Bridgetown is Barbados's capital and largest city.

The Fenty family did not have much money, so Ronald supplemented the family income by working as a street vendor selling clothing. When she wasn't in school, Robyn helped her father sometimes and even set up her own little stall selling hats, scarves, and belts. She also bought candy and packaged it, reselling it at a profit to friends at school. But Robyn didn't start her own business just for fun. Her family needed extra money, because her father had some expensive and dangerous addictions: drugs and alcohol.

A STRESSFUL HOME

Robyn's home life was stressful. Her parents often argued, and their marriage was unstable. Even though he loved his family, Ronald hurt them by spending a lot of time and money getting high and drinking. Sometimes he would even turn violent and physically abuse Robyn's mother.

Robyn was a shy child who didn't act out her feelings with tantrums or crying. Instead, she repressed her feelings of sadness and anger. But keeping her emotions bottled up had a negative impact on Robyn's health, and when she was only eight years old, she began getting headaches. Her mother took her to doctors, but for years they were unable to determine what was wrong. The doctors thought she might have a brain tumor, but tests and scans revealed there was no physical cause for the headaches.

One day when Robyn was only nine years old, she walked into a room and saw her father smoking crack cocaine. Shortly after the incident, Ronald left home, and Monica had to support her family by herself.

> "I was really young when I was living with [my dad's] addictions. I didn't understand exactly . . . but I knew he was doing something he shouldn't be doing. Even when I started to understand, I looked up to my dad so much that I couldn't put him and this negative thing together. At the time there was no way I could help him out of it."[1]
>
> —*RIHANNA*

Monica worked long hours as an accountant to make ends meet. This meant Robyn had to take care of herself and her brothers while their mom worked. But Robyn didn't resent this early responsibility—she accepted it as a reality she had to deal with.

Monica and Ronald broke up and reunited several times throughout Robyn's childhood. Finally, when Robyn was 14, her parents got a divorce. With Robyn's father gone from the house for good, her home life became much more stable, which helped her headaches disappear.

ESCAPING THROUGH MUSIC

Robyn also experienced stress in other areas of life. Because of her light skin and green eyes, classmates bullied Robyn and called her "white."[2] Some Barbadians are prejudiced toward lighter-skinned people and trust only those with African features and skin coloring. Barbadians are proud of their African heritage and celebrate it, but sometimes take it too far by discriminating against those who don't appear black enough.

Being called "white" in a nation proud of its black heritage was difficult for Robyn. But she grew to be tough and not let the bullies know they hurt her feelings. She learned to be strong and confident in her own identity.

From age seven, Robyn found comfort from her troubles in singing. Like many little girls,

CARIBBEAN MUSIC

Calypso is a musical style that evolved in the Caribbean after African slaves were brought to the islands. Because slave masters didn't allow slaves to speak with one another, the slaves sang and drummed as a way to communicate. They also used music to mock their slave masters, so traditional calypso usually involves humorous satire.

Robyn loved singing and dreamed of becoming a performer.

Robyn loved to sing. She would pretend she was performing in front of an audience, holding her hairbrush like a microphone or a broom like a microphone stand. Her next-door neighbors could hear her practicing. One neighbor, Dawn Johnson, said they "used to call her Robyn Red Breast because she was always singing like a bird."[3]

Robyn grew up listening mostly to reggae, but she was exposed to a wide variety of Caribbean-style music such as calypso, soca, and ringbang. She also enjoyed hip-hop, R&B, and American pop music she heard in clubs and movies. One of her biggest influences was singer Mariah Carey. Robyn identified closely with the singer because, like Robyn, Carey was young, biracial, and loved to sing. She also liked singers Whitney Houston and Beyoncé.

FINDING HER OWN WAY

Robyn went to secondary school at Combermere High School. When she was 13, she joined the Barbados Cadet Corps, a government-sponsored program to establish discipline and good among young people over the age of 12. Robyn went on weekend excursions with the cadets, where she learned military discipline. "Uniforms had to be spick and span, our boots had to shine like diamonds, and we'd often need to cook for the entire camp," Robyn said.[4] Robyn's favorite part of the cadets was learning to shoot a pistol. "I was a good shot, although I couldn't kill a fly from a hundred paces," Robyn said.[5]

Staying in the cadets meant Robyn would have to stay in school and graduate. But Robyn wasn't sure she was cut out to be a student. She didn't like studying and she didn't get along with the teachers. Sometimes she even skipped school and spent all day at the beach. Her desire to sing and perform was growing stronger than anything else.

Robyn continued to pursue her dream of having a music career. When she was 15, Robyn invited two of her classmates to join her in forming a girls singing group. It would be the first important step in making her dreams come true.

|||||||||||

DRILL SERGEANT SHONTELLE

When Robyn was in the Barbados Cadet Corps, she had a drill sergeant named Shontelle Layne. Shontelle later became a pop singer, and in 2008 she released the song "T-Shirt," which reached Number 1 on *Billboard*'s Dance/Club Play song chart. "[Robyn] was a good cadet . . . though there was one occasion when I had to make her drop and give me ten push-ups," Shontelle said. "We laugh about it now. I think she's forgiven me."[6]

A chance audition for a tourist sparked Robyn's music career.

CHAPTER 3

Rising Star

||||||||||||||||||||||||||||||||||||||||||||||||||||||||||||||||||||||||||

Barbados is a vacation destination for tourists all over the world. Native Barbadians also return to visit their island home after moving away, including Jackie Jordan. A Barbadian, Jordan married New York-based record producer Evan Rogers and often returned to visit Barbados.

One day in late 2003, Jordan, Rogers, and their family were talking with a friend who also happened to be friends with the Fenty family. The friend told Rogers about Robyn and her singing group. It wasn't uncommon for Rogers, a well-known record producer and songwriter, to have someone begging him for an audition. But Robyn's friend must have convinced him, because he agreed to audition the trio.

Wearing pink capri pants, a pink shirt, and sneakers, Robyn and her trio met Rogers and Jordan at their hotel. Rogers said he saw something special in Robyn. "She had this incredible presence," Rogers said.[1] "It was like the other two girls didn't exist."[2] The girls sang "Emotion," a song by female singing group Destiny's Child. Afterward, Rogers asked only Robyn to come back for a second audition and bring her mother.

CHARTING A STAR PATH

Robyn took her mother to meet with Rogers, this time auditioning solo. Although Robyn's voice was "a little rough around the edges . . . she had this edge to [it]," Rogers said.[3] Rogers knew he could help her develop her voice. He immediately noticed Robyn had a rare combination of qualities with star potential: natural beauty, a good singing voice, and a poised and confident presence. Even at age 15, Robyn was stunning. Rogers and Monica began planning for Robyn's future.

Typically, the first step in getting a record deal is recording a demo, which helps generate interest in a new song or performer. So in 2004, Rogers and his friend and business partner Carl Sturken brought Robyn and her mother to the United States. They wanted to help Robyn develop her voice and image and record a demo.

> "I knew she had something really special and I thought if we could get her a record deal, she could do something."[4]
>
> —EVAN ROGERS

Although Robyn wanted to focus on her potential music career full time, Monica said she had to stay in school until she officially signed a recording contract. So over school holidays, summer, and winter breaks, Robyn and her mom traveled between Barbados and Rogers's studio in Stamford, Connecticut.

Rogers, *left*, and Sturken, *right*, saw Robyn's potential as a future star.

In 2004, Robyn signed a contract with Rogers and Sturken's production company, Syndicated Rhythm Productions (SRP), and she was given her own manager and lawyer. Rogers and Sturken selected several demo songs for Robyn. These included the Whitney Houston song "For the Love of You," a ballad they had cowritten, titled "Last Time," and an upbeat Caribbean-style song called "Pon de Replay." In January 2005, after a year of hard work and preparation, Robyn and her first demo record were ready to meet the music industry.

SIGNING WITH DEF JAM

While Rogers and Sturken sent the demo to various record companies, Robyn flew back to Barbados. She thought it would be months before she heard any news. But just three days later, Rogers called her and said, "Jay Z wants to meet you."[5] Hip-hop star Shawn "Jay Z" Carter had just become the new president and chief executive officer (CEO) of Def Jam Records.

EVAN ROGERS AND CARL STURKEN

Evan Rogers and Carl Sturken have worked as musicians, songwriters, and producers in the music industry since the 1980s. They wrote and produced several songs for Christina Aguilera's debut album, which sold more than 11 million copies worldwide. They have also written hits for Jessica Simpson, Mandy Moore, Anastacia, *NSYNC, Shontelle, and Kelly Clarkson. In 2005 they created their own record label, Syndicated Rhythm Productions (SRP). Rihanna was the first artist they signed.

Two days later, Robyn was incredibly nervous and shaking as she waited in the Def Jam lobby. When Jay Z invited her into his office for the audition, music executive Antonio "L. A." Reid and other Def Jam executives were there. Despite her trembling nerves, she became calm as soon as she began singing "For the Love of You." "I remember staring into everybody's eyes in the room while

JAY Z

Jay Z was born Shawn Corey Carter in 1969, in Brooklyn, New York. When Carter was 11, his father abandoned his family, leaving his mother, Gloria Carter, alone to raise her four children in a drug-infested neighborhood. Carter's teen years were rough. He was involved with drug dealing and gun violence but dreamed of a better life. Rap music became his escape.

After teaming up with an older rapper named Jaz-O in 1989, Carter changed his name to Jay-Z, later Jay Z. He worked hard for many years, but no record companies were interested in signing him. So, in 1996, Jay Z and two friends started their own record label, Roc-A-Fella Records, which no longer exists. In 1996, Jay Z recorded and released his first album, *Reasonable Doubt*, which is now considered a hip-hop classic.

The talented rapper has since released many successful albums and is one of the most highly respected names in the music industry. In 2008, Jay Z married singer Beyoncé Knowles. They have one daughter, Blue Ivy Carter.

Jay Z is a successful rapper, record executive, and businessman.

I was singing, and at that point, I was fearless," Robyn said. "But the minute I stopped singing, I was like, 'Oh my God, Jay Z is sitting right in front of me.'"[6]

Jay Z and Reid were both impressed by Robyn's beauty and confidence. "It took me two minutes to see she was a star," Jay Z said.[7] They found the fierce determination in Robyn's eyes the most impressive. According to Reid, her eyes said, "I'm gonna make it."[8] Jay Z and Reid wanted to sign Robyn immediately. Jay Z wouldn't let anyone leave until the contract was signed.

The lawyers negotiated her contract for hours while Robyn waited nervously. Finally, around 3:00 a.m., a deal had been made: Robyn was officially a Def Jam artist with a contract to produce six albums.

ROBYN TO RIHANNA

The next thing Robyn had to do was choose a stage name. There was already a Swedish singer

DEF JAM RECORDS

Record producer Rick Rubin and his friend Russell Simmons founded Def Jam Records as an independent record label out of his college dorm room at New York University in 1984. Def Jam first found success with releases from rapper LL Cool J, including his song "I Need a Beat" in 1984. In 1985, Def Jam produced and released "Rock Hard" by hip-hop trio the Beastie Boys. The Beastie Boys are often credited with helping rap music become more mainstream. Def Jam eventually became one of the top recording companies in hip-hop and urban music.

> "Robyn is the brick to my foundation. It's something I hold on to. It's everything I grew up with, my childhood, Barbados, people close to me. Everything that's familiar. People know Rihanna from my music. But if this were to all go away tomorrow, I would always look at myself as Robyn."[9]
>
> —*RIHANNA*

named Robyn. So Robyn chose to use her middle name, Rihanna, as her professional name. But her family and close friends would always know her as Robyn.

Rogers and Jordan invited Rihanna to live with them in New York City while she worked on her first album. Monica needed to stay in Barbados, so she agreed to allow them to be her daughter's temporary guardians. The next morning, Rihanna went shopping in New York City for an entirely new wardrobe.

It is very rare to audition as an unknown artist for a record company and sign a huge contract in one day. But Rihanna was about to show everyone she wasn't any ordinary young woman.

||||||||||

Rihanna's first single, "Pon de Replay," became the hit of the summer in 2005.

CHAPTER 4

Flying as Rihanna

||||||||||||||||||||||||||||||||||||||||||||||||

ow that Rihanna had signed with Def Jam Records, the record company set out to create an image and sound for her as she appeared to the public. Def Jam paid her well for the right to turn her into the kind of artist they thought would make her successful in the music industry. This meant they would choose her hairstyle, makeup, clothes, and songs

In a 2009 interview, Rihanna talked about the first time she realized she was famous. "I was in a New York studio finishing my album and popped out to the ice cream store on the corner," she said. "As I was walking out with my strawberry ice cream, six or seven kids got up off their seats and ran towards me with napkins to sign. That was weird for me."[1]

for her. Rihanna had no control over how she was presented to the public at the time.

Because Rihanna was from the Caribbean, Def Jam decided to market her music to a reggae-friendly audience. Her debut album would be titled *Music of the Sun*, and would include not only reggae styles, but also hip-hop, R&B, and dancehall songs. Jay Z had already decided her first single would be the Caribbean-dancehall style song "Pon de Replay." He was sure it would be a hit and convince radio listeners to buy Rihanna's first album when it was released.

Not long after Def Jam released her first single in the summer of 2005, Rihanna was at a shopping mall. She heard "Pon de Replay" played for the first time on the radio. This was the first time she had heard herself outside the studio. Rihanna was so excited she "ran up and down screaming, 'That's my song!'"[2] Strangers stared at her like there was something wrong with her, but Rihanna didn't care.

"Pon de Replay" soared almost to the top of the *Billboard* charts, reaching Number 2. The single was a summer 2005 dance club favorite across the United States. When *Music of the Sun* hit store shelves in August, fans were eager to buy it. *Music of the Sun* sold more than 500,000 copies nationally and climbed to *Billboard*'s Number 10 spot, earning Rihanna her first gold album award from the Recording Industry Association of America (RIAA). It was a wonderful start to the singer's career.

PON DE REPLAY

Pon de replay is Caribbean slang for "upon the replay." The lyrics, "Come mister DJ, song pon de replay," really mean, "Hey, DJ, replay that song." The first time Rihanna heard the song, she thought it sounded "sing-songy and . . . nursery-rhymish."[3] But she had no choice in the matter, so she decided to have fun with it.

A GIRL LIKE ME

Less than a month after *Music of the Sun* was released, Rihanna was back in the studio making her next album. Because Rihanna's first album sold well, it was decided *A Girl Like Me* would feature similar song styles. But this time, Rihanna had more input on the album and her music. She chose the album title and cowrote three songs on the album: "Kisses Don't Lie," "Break It Off," and "A Girl Like Me." She also suggested adding some rock and roll into her music and chose to work with songwriter Ne-Yo.

While she was developing her second album, Rihanna also continued to promote her first one. Between recordings, she flew around the country to perform in live shows. She also toured for a while, performing as the opening act for singer Gwen Stefani. It was a busy schedule, but Rihanna was doing what she loved.

"SOS" SUCCESS

Rihanna's first single from *A Girl Like Me*, "SOS," was released in early 2006 and sailed to the top

PERSONALLY SPEAKING

Rihanna's second album, *A Girl Like Me*, was a much more personal album for her than *Music of the Sun*. She said each song spoke in some way about what it was like to be a girl like her:

"Whether I've been cheated on, falling in and out of love, people hating on me . . . that crazy feeling guys give you, partying—every aspect of my life."[4]

Rihanna promoted her album on MTV's "Total Request Live" in April 2006.

of the *Billboard* charts. It became Rihanna's first Number 1 hit and stayed in the top spot for three weeks. Three different music videos were made for the song, including the official music video and two promos for clothing companies Agent Provocateur and Nike. This introduced Rihanna to the world of commercial endorsements.

A Girl Like Me was released on April 25, 2006. Although it was a commercial success, many critics bashed it for including heavy, adult-themed ballads inappropriate for a teenage singer. While some critics enjoyed "SOS," they didn't like the ballads, especially "Unfaithful," with one critic calling Rihanna's vocals "horsey."[5] They described the melodramatic lyrics, which compared cheating to murder, as just plain "weird."[6]

But Rihanna's fans didn't seem to pay attention to what critics were saying. They liked "Unfaithful" enough to put it into the Top 10 around the world. "Break It Off" also made it into the Top 10. By the summer of 2006, Rihanna was so successful Def Jam decided it was time to send her on tour, headlining her own act.

"SOS"

"SOS" was used in the film sound track for *Bring It On: All or Nothing*. Rihanna made a cameo as herself in the 2006 film, marking her first onscreen appearance.

"SOS" was also used in the 2011 film *Alvin and the Chipmunks: Chipwrecked*, recorded by animated singing group the Chipettes.

Rihanna's second album, *A Girl Like Me*, debuted at Number 5 on the *Billboard* 200 album chart.

RIHANNA: LIVE IN CONCERT TOUR

For her first tour, Rihanna performed 36 shows from July to September 2006 throughout North America. Promoting both *Music of the Sun* (2005) and *A Girl like Me* (2006), she performed songs from both albums. That fall she toured as a guest performer with the Pussycat Dolls, Jay Z, Ne-Yo, and the Black Eyed Peas.

A Girl Like Me sold more than 1.3 million copies and earned Rihanna her first platinum award from the RIAA. Rihanna's second album was one of the Top 20 best-selling albums worldwide for 2006. People loved her image as an adorable island girl—but Rihanna was about to shake up her image for good.

‖‖‖‖‖‖

Rihanna changed her carefully crafted image by cutting her hair in late 2006.

CHAPTER 5

Good Girl Gone Bad

||||||||||||||||||||||||||||||||||||||||||||||||||||||||||||||

N ot long after Rihanna's popularity grew, she became the target of critics and tabloids. Some ridiculed her as "the Bajan Beyoncé," suggesting Rihanna was imitating the older pop star's style.[1]

A rumor also circulated about her having an affair with Jay Z, which explained why he signed her with Def Jam. At the time, Jay Z was dating

Beyoncé. At first Rihanna laughed it off, but the gossip persisted, even claiming Rihanna and Beyoncé were fighting over Jay Z.

In reality, Jay Z was more like a mentor to Rihanna. Over time, Rihanna learned to ignore such gossip.

CHANGING IT UP

In late 2006, Rihanna was in Paris, France, and decided she wanted to change her hairstyle. "I had my long locks cut off and came away with this cute bob that I was really happy with," she said.[2] But Def Jam executives told her while the haircut looked good, it didn't work with her image. They told her she would need to wear hair extensions. "I was completely crushed," Rihanna said. "That's when I realized things had to change."[3]

Rihanna wanted to express more of herself in her music, style, and performances—and not the innocent image others were forcing onto her. She also knew to stay at the top of the music charts she would have to widen her audience from reggae and dancehall music to more popular fare.

BRANDY'S AFRODISIAC

R&B singer Brandy earned a 2004 Grammy Award for Best Contemporary R&B Album for *Afrodisiac*. Nekesa Mumbi Moody of the Associated Press wrote *Afrodisiac* "was surely [Brandy's] best . . . this album captures your attention from the first note and refuses to be ignored."[5] In addition to inspiring Rihanna's *Good Girl Gone Bad*, Brandy's music has also influenced other musicians including Beyoncé, Ciara, and Keyshia Cole.

GOOD GIRL GONE BAD

For her third album, Rihanna drew inspiration from *Afrodisiac*, the 2004 album by singer Brandy Norwood. Rihanna listened to the entire album over and over, loving every song. She wanted to make an album like it—one filled with great songs "that people could listen to from beginning to end, without skipping any [songs]," Rihanna said.[4] Her new goal was to make her next album as good as *Afrodisiac*.

Rihanna planned her third album carefully. She wanted to record a variety of song styles, so she chose heartfelt ballads and up-tempo songs with danceable rhythms. She collaborated with other artists such as Jay Z, Ne-Yo, and Justin

Rihanna has used umbrellas as props when performing her hit single "Umbrella."

Timberlake on performances and songwriting for the album. Rihanna wanted this new album to be edgy and more mature. She began taking charge of her career.

Good Girl Gone Bad was recorded during late 2006 and early 2007. The album contained several hits, including "Shut Up and Drive," "Don't Stop the Music," and "Hate That I Love You." Leading up to the album's May 2007 release, Def Jam put out the single "Umbrella," which features Jay Z. "Umbrella" would make Rihanna a superstar.

SUMMER OF UMBRELLAS

Once "Umbrella" hit the airwaves in March 2007, it became an instant international hit. It held the Number 1 spot on US charts for ten weeks. In the United Kingdom, it spent 11 weeks at Number 1. Fans couldn't wait to buy the album. In the first

"Bad is not sleazy. [It] just means I've gotten a little rebellious . . . broken out of my shell . . . I basically took the attitude of the bad girl and . . . did everything the way I wanted to do it. I just reinvented myself . . . It's all about the attitude that you take toward things . . . I'm taking risks, because bad girls take risks."[6]

—RIHANNA

week alone, more than 162,000 copies of *Good Girl Gone Bad* were sold in the United States.

Def Jam further capitalized on the song's success by partnering with the manufacturer Totes to launch a line of umbrellas, which were available at Macy's department stores beginning in the summer of 2007. The Rihanna-style umbrellas were immensely popular and increased Totes's sales tremendously. Fans even brought umbrellas to her concerts and opened them as Rihanna sang the lyrics, "You can stand under my umbrella, ella, ella . . ."[7]

The worldwide success of "Umbrella" also coincided with the wettest June on record for

SYMBOLS AND SUPERSTITION

"Umbrella" uses metaphors, which can be interpreted in different ways. "An umbrella is protection, it protects you from rain," Rihanna said. "The rain, in this case, is negativeness and vulnerability."[8] Most listeners interpreted "Umbrella" as a song about protecting loved ones from harm of any kind.

An old superstition claims it is bad luck to open an umbrella indoors. Rihanna believed this superstition, but changed her mind when she started working on the music video for "Umbrella." For Rihanna, singing and dancing indoors with an open umbrella brought her very good luck.

the United Kingdom. It was warm and sunny in the country the day the single was released. But the next day, as "Umbrella" sales skyrocketed, severe storms hit the British Isles, with flash flood warnings and torrential downpours. Some people jokingly blamed Rihanna's hit song for causing the storms.

SHOWERED WITH PRAISE

Rihanna's Good Girl Gone Bad Tour lasted for 15 months, from September 2007 through December 2008. She performed approximately 80 concerts around the world. Meanwhile, *Good Girl Gone Bad* earned her several nominations for music industry awards. In November, Rihanna won the AMA for Favorite Soul/R&B Female Artist at the AMAs in Los Angeles, beating out Beyoncé and Fantasia.

At the 2008 Grammy Awards on February 10, 2008, Rihanna performed her singles "Umbrella" and "Don't Stop the Music." She was also nominated for four Grammys: Best Dance Recording for "Don't Stop the Music," Best R&B Performance by a Duo or Group with Vocals for "Hate That I Love You" with Ne-Yo,

Rihanna won her first Grammy in 2008 for her collaboration on "Umbrella" with Jay Z.

Rihanna loves dressing up and creating new looks. "The thrill in fashion for me is taking a risk and daring myself to make it work," she told *Seventeen*. "I always buy something twisted . . . I know I'm going to have to figure out [how] to pull it off and make it my own."[10]

Rihanna wasn't always the glamorous celebrity she is today. During an interview, Rihanna admitted to being a tomboy when she was a little girl. Although she became interested in makeup and clothes in her teens, she still enjoys being a tomboy sometimes. She even prefers hanging out with men, thinking they offer better conversation than women.

and both Record of the Year and Best Rap/Sung Collaboration for "Umbrella."

Rihanna took home the Grammy for Best Rap/Sung Collaboration for "Umbrella," becoming the first Barbadian woman to win a Grammy. The prime minister of Barbados even called to congratulate the singer after her win.

In the summer of 2007, Rihanna was featured as the new face of CoverGirl cosmetics. "I always wanted to be a CoverGirl. Every little girl wants to become one," she said.[9] As the face of CoverGirl, Rihanna appeared in television commercials, magazine advertisements, and billboards.

BAD GIRL DOING GOOD

Rihanna had also spent time on charity work in 2008. In 2006, she founded the BELIEVE Foundation, a charity committed to raising awareness about the impact of blood cancers such as leukemia. The foundation says it works to provide youth with "educational, financial, social and medical support when and wherever it is needed."[11]

In support of her foundation, Rihanna performed minitours with short concerts during the spring of 2008. These concerts raised money and helped recruit bone marrow donors for people fighting leukemia. Rihanna's goal for her foundation was not only to help kids fighting cancer but also to make sure they were happy, so they could believe in life.

At the end of 2008, Rihanna was also asked to perform at the Feeding America and RIAA Presidential Inauguration Charity Ball. Held in honor of President Barack Obama's January 20, 2009, inauguration, the event helped raise money and awareness about hunger among millions of starving families across America.

As a performer, Rihanna has participated in several charity events, including her own BELIEVE Foundation

After finding success in 2008, Rihanna was looking forward to the release of her *Good Girl Gone Bad: Reloaded* remix album, which included some new singles. It looked like 2009 would be another record-breaking year for Rihanna. She had no idea it would be heartbreaking as well.

||||||||||

Rihanna and Chris Brown were both rising stars when they performed at Z100's Jingle Ball in 2005.

CHAPTER 6

Disturbing
Events

IIIIIIIIIIIIIIIIIIIIIIIIIIIIIIIIIIIIIIIIIII

ihanna had been friends with singer Chris Brown since 2005. Despite rumors of romance in the media, they both said they were just close friends. Photos were published of the two hanging out, suggesting they were much more than just "buddies" or collaborators.[1] Finally, in 2008, Rihanna and Brown admitted they were dating.

Brown had written Rihanna's 2008 hit song "Disturbia," which came out in June 2008. He had originally intended to perform the song, but presented it to Rihanna instead. When she heard the demo, she decided to record "Disturbia" and include it on her remix album, *Good Girl Gone Bad: Reloaded*. It turned out to be a smart move. The song climbed to Number 1 on the *Billboard* Hot 100.

In December 2008, Rihanna and some of her family spent Christmas with Brown's family in Virginia. It seemed like their relationship was becoming serious. As the 2009 Grammy Awards approached, Rihanna and Brown had a lot to look forward to. Both were nominated and scheduled to perform. "Disturbia" was nominated for Best Dance Recording, so if it won, it would be a win for both of them. But something very different happened on February 8, 2009, the day of the awards.

LOVE TURNS DANGEROUS

Rihanna and Brown canceled their appearances just a few hours before the Grammys. At first, both said they had been in a car accident. But eventually

Rihanna and Brown attended a pre-Grammy dinner together the night before he assaulted her.

the truth about the couple's abrupt cancellation emerged. Rihanna was in the hospital being treated for injuries, while Brown had turned himself into the police for attacking and physically beating her.

The official Los Angeles Police report stated Rihanna and Brown were in a car together when Brown received a text message from his former girlfriend inviting him to come over. Rihanna read the text, which led to an argument with Brown,

LOVE OR OBSESSION

who tried to push her out of the car. He then slammed her head against the passenger window and repeatedly punched her with his right hand while steering the car with his left. When Rihanna tried calling a friend for help, Brown threw her phone out the car window and threatened to kill her. Rihanna tried using Brown's cell phone to send a text for help, but he put her in a headlock and bit her when she attempted to get free. Finally, Brown stopped the car and fled while Rihanna screamed for help. Bystanders overheard her cries, called 911, and waited with her until the police arrived. Brown later turned himself in to authorities.

In an interview months later, Rihanna would say Brown became someone else when he attacked her. She said, "It wasn't the same person that says I love you . . . He had . . . no soul in his eyes . . . He was clearly blacked out. There was no person when I looked at him."[3]

AFTERMATH AND RECOVERY

Although Rihanna was left bloody and badly bruised by Brown's assault, she didn't press charges against him. Brown turned himself in and eventually pleaded guilty to two felony charges. The judge sentenced Brown to five years probation, six months of community service, and one year of domestic violence counseling. A restraining order also required Brown to stay 150 feet (46 m) from Rihanna, or 30 feet (9 m) away from her at a public event. Many radio stations stopped playing Brown's music and his tour was canceled in 2010.

The day after the attack, the media chaos was intense. Helicopters circled Rihanna's house, and reporters crowded her street. She couldn't even go home until things quieted down.

Many fans were shocked when Rihanna and Brown went on vacation together just weeks after he assaulted her. Rihanna had been scared, lonely, and depressed following the incident, and she missed the closeness she had with Brown. She wanted everything to be the way it was before the incident.

Rihanna told ABC's Diane Sawyer she was in denial even after the physical wounds faded. She said she started lying to herself, putting the traumatizing experience in the back of her mind and not facing the reality of what happened. That was how she was able to briefly reunite with Brown.

Rihanna said she believed she had to protect Brown from the judgment of the world. She worried for his safety and even began blaming herself for the attack. But Rihanna couldn't keep lying to herself, so not long after the March trip, she broke up with Brown. "I can't see how we . . . would get back together, but . . . I can't predict the future," she said.[5]

Rihanna remained out of the public eye for a few weeks while she healed from her injuries. A spokesperson for Rihanna issued a public statement saying, "[Rihanna] wants to assure her fans that she remains strong, is doing well, and deeply appreciates the outpouring of support she has received during this difficult time."[4]

Unfortunately, a photo taken by police on the night of the assault showing Rihanna's battered and swollen face was leaked to the media. Soon the photo was splashed all over the Internet. "It was humiliating; that is not a photo you would show to anybody," Rihanna later said. "I felt completely taken advantage of. I felt like people were making it into a fun topic on the Internet, and it's my life."[6]

The love of family and close friends helped Rihanna recover from the incident. Music was also another important piece of Rihanna's healing process. About a month after the attack, she went to work on a new album. It was edgier and angrier than anything Rihanna had done thus far. The new album was *Rated R*.

MAKING *RATED R*

Once again, Rihanna teamed up with several writers and producers, including Ne-Yo and Justin Timberlake, to create her fourth studio album. But this time, she wrote many of the lyrics herself. She wanted this album to say just what she wanted to say, even if people didn't like it.

The assault and its aftermath had a major influence on Rihanna's music in *Rated R.*

The album's first single was "Russian Roulette," a song comparing a romantic relationship to a deadly game of chance. Another successful single off the album was "Rude Boy," in which she taunts a boyfriend, questioning his masculinity. In the songs "Photographs" and "Cold Case Love," she surveys the damage of broken relationships.

"Stupid in Love" is about getting tricked by a lover and living to regret it.

Critics gave *Rated R* mixed reviews when it was released in November 2009. But it seemed they all agreed on one thing: the songs were heavily influenced by Rihanna's relationship with Brown. About the album, one critic said it is "impossible not to hear the anger and hurt in her voice."[7] But the overall impression was *Rated R* made an honest statement about the conflicting emotions a woman feels after someone she has loved and trusted abuses her. One critic said Rihanna "turned . . . regret into powerful and moving art."[8]

For Rihanna, making *Rated R* was a creative catharsis. After getting it out of her system, she decided her next albums would express the fun and rowdy side of life.

||||||||||

ON THE REBOUND ||||||||||||||||||||||||||||||||||||||||||||||||||||||||||||||||||||

Rihanna was hesitant to date again after the trauma she experienced in 2009. But in 2010, she began dating Matt Kemp, an outfielder for the Los Angeles Dodgers. The two were together as much as possible for a while, but Rihanna was often away promoting her music, so Kemp started seeing other women. After a few months of dating, Rihanna and Kemp broke up.

Rihanna performed during the Hope for Haiti Now telethon.

CHAPTER 7

Loud and Proud

n January 12, 2010, a massive earthquake struck the Caribbean island of Haiti, killing more than 200,000 people and leaving most of the nation without clean water or sanitation. People were homeless, dying of starvation and thirst, and contracting illnesses. Rihanna quickly joined many other celebrities to raise money for Haiti during the Hope for Haiti Now telethon live from London, England.

Just ten days after the earthquake, Rihanna, Jay Z, and singer Bono performed a new song, "Stranded (Haiti Mon Amour)," live on international television. Jay Z rapped a prayer while Rihanna and Bono sang, "Can't wait until tomorrow . . . Not gonna leave you stranded."[1]

The telethon and advance sales of the live album *Hope for Haiti Now* raised more than $58 million in the first 48 hours. The album includes Christina Aguilera, Alicia Keys, Beyoncé, Stevie Wonder, and Bruce Springsteen.

DOING HER THING

Ten days after the telethon, Rihanna was on stage in Los Angeles accepting the 2010 Grammy for Best Rap/Sung Collaboration with Jay Z and rapper Kanye West for the single "Run This Town." It was

CARIBBEAN FAMILY

Rihanna felt a strong bond with the Haitian people when the 2010 earthquake struck Haiti. To her, when the earthquake struck Haiti, it felt like it happened to Barbados. "In the Caribbean, we think of ourselves as one big family, one country," Rihanna said. "We're all together. We all represent each other."[2]

Rihanna took home another Grammy in 2010.

her second Grammy win. Then it was back to the studio to plan and record her next album: *Loud*.

Rihanna knew exactly what she wanted on her fourth album: fun and upbeat songs on an album filled with potential hit singles. To meet this goal, Def Jam recruited approximately 50 songwriters and producers to come up with 200 songs in two weeks. Then, Rihanna and her team eventually chose 11 favorites from the pool of offerings.

The lead single was "Only Girl (in the World)," which reached Number 1 on the *Billboard* Hot 100 and went platinum. Rihanna's collaboration with rapper Drake on the song "What's My Name?" also went platinum.

Once again, Rihanna was in the middle of a hectic schedule. She was balancing recording sessions for *Loud* with performances around the world for her Last Girl on Earth Tour. The tour launched in April 2010 to promote *Rated R* in North America, Europe, and Australia. The 67-show tour was the most lavish and daring production Rihanna had ever done.

A RAUNCHY EXAMPLE

By the time *Loud* was released in November 2010, several of its singles had already climbed to the top of the charts. *Loud* debuted at Number 3 on the *Billboard* 200 chart and sold 1.5 million copies in the United States. But not all listeners were pleased with the theme of Rihanna's latest music, particularly her song "S&M." Some songs considered too inappropriate for young listeners were censored for radio and YouTube. Critics said Rihanna was a negative role model for girls, saying her image had gone beyond bad girl and had become raunchy.

In an interview with *Vogue* in April 2011, Rihanna responded to the criticism. She said,

BAD AT THE BRITS

The first British Record Industry Awards, nicknamed the Brit Awards, were held in 1977. Similar to the Grammy Awards, the Brit Awards are televised live with glitzy musical performances and an awards ceremony.

In 2011, Rihanna was nominated for a Brit Award. She was also scheduled to perform "The Only Girl (in the World)," "What's My Name?," and "S&M" but was strictly warned to sanitize the overtly sexual lyrics and dance movements. British station Radio 1 had already refused to play "S&M," and the song's music video was also banned in 11 countries.

This didn't make Rihanna very happy. Other than changing some of the questionable lyrics, she didn't really clean up the song. Many people thought the performance was still too raunchy for a television audience. Despite the controversy, Rihanna came back on stage, wearing a beautiful white dress with red flowers, and graciously received her Brit Award for Best International Female Solo Artist.

I definitely want to help and teach little girls whenever I can. But then there is a character that I have to play in my videos to tell stories. And a lot of the parts that I play aren't necessarily what I stand for in real life.[3]

BATTLESHIP DEBUT

Film director Peter Berg was attracted to Rihanna's tough yet playful bad-girl attitude in 2010. Berg was looking for an actress to play a female Navy officer in his new movie, *Battleship,* and thought Rihanna would be perfect for the role.

Filming for *Battleship* began in September 2010 in Hawaii. Rihanna was thrilled to be part of the action, even though she spent up to six hours a day in a rubber raft pretending to shoot a large machine gun. The water was choppy, with ridges up to seven feet (2 m) and sharks swimming nearby. "There were all these people, cameras, and huge cranes out in the middle of the ocean," Rihanna said. "And I got to do some stunts, which was incredible. I loved it—especially diving into the ocean."[4]

Rihanna drew on her Cadet Corps experience for her role in *Battleship*.

Battleship opened in theaters in May 2012, but it turned out to be an expensive flop at the box office. Reviews criticized its ridiculous plot and poorly written dialogue. However, Rihanna did her best with her first role on the big screen. Berg said it would position her to do more films in the future.

Rihanna gave two electric performances at the 2011 Grammy Awards.

WORKING TOO HARD

In February 2011, Rihanna performed twice at the Grammy Awards, this time in two duets: "What's My Name?" with Drake and "Love the Way You Lie" with Eminem. She also won Best Dance Recording for "Only Girl (in the World)" and was nominated for Song of the Year and Record of the Year for "Love the Way You Lie."

Between June and December 2011, Rihanna performed 98 shows for the Loud Tour. She also continued a hectic studio schedule, recording her sixth album, *Talk That Talk*, only ten months after releasing *Loud*.

Talk That Talk was recorded in studios in 25 different cities and countries around the world, including Paris, London, Denmark, and Germany. Once Rihanna finished a concert performance, she would go directly to a studio to record, and then board her tour bus to the next concert city. Eventually, she was hospitalized for exhaustion while touring in Sweden. Rihanna blamed it on the flu virus, even posting a photo to Twitter of an IV in her arm as proof.

Rihanna released *Talk That Talk* on November 18, 2011. It was another album full of hits. She once again drew criticism for her raunchy and sexual lyrics. Whether or not critics liked her songs, Rihanna would continue her reputation as a dominator of the pop music charts.

||||||||||

"LOVE THE WAY YOU LIE"

When Eminem wrote the lyrics to "Love the Way You Lie," he had Rihanna in mind. Eminem has had his own experience with domestic violence. The song is an expression of what gets lovers into a cycle of violence and what keeps them there—and both parties are portrayed as active participants.

Rihanna performed "We Found Love" at the 2012 Grammy Awards.

CHAPTER 8

Life in the Spotlight

||||||||||||||||||||||||||||||||||||||||||||||||||||

A t the 2012 Grammy Awards in February, buzz circled around Rihanna once again. Surrounded by dancers, she gave an upbeat performance of her single "We Found Love." She also sang with British rock band Coldplay during a performance of their hit song "Princess of China." Then she received more acclaim: another Grammy for her collaboration on the song "All of the Lights." People talked

In March 2012, Rihanna released a remix and video of her hit "Birthday Cake," this time featuring Brown— and Brown remixed his song "Turn Up the Music," featuring Rihanna. Although she claimed it was just an innocent musical trade-off for the sake of their fans and they weren't back together romantically, it made observers question those claims.

about her win, her performances, and the amazing Armani outfit she wore. But they seemed most fascinated with the rumor she and Brown were getting back together.

During an August 2012 interview with Oprah Winfrey, Rihanna said she had forgiven Brown, who had also been the victim of abuse. Believing he should be given the chance to change, she said she still loved him and probably always would. Rihanna also opened up and tearfully expressed how painful it was to lose Brown, her best friend, after the February 2009 incident.

UNAPOLOGETIC PERSONAL LIFE

Rihanna started gearing up for her seventh album, *Unapologetic*, in June 2012. Once again, she recruited big name songwriters and producers, such as Ne-Yo, Terius Nash, and David Guetta. Rihanna spent weeks working on the music, often spending all night in the studio.

> "I named my album *Unapologetic* because there is only one truth, and you can't apologize for that. It's honest. I'm always evolving of course. I think the only motto I have is to be true to myself."[1]
>
> —RIHANNA

In an interview on Facebook Live, Rihanna said "Nobody's Business" expresses how she views her personal life. Even though so much of her life is documented and treated like public property, it is still her life. Who she dates and other private information are things she wants to keep to herself. She was asked if releasing songs such as "Nobody's Business" invited people to comment on her life decisions. She said,

Stockholm, Sweden, was one of the stops on Rihanna's
777 Tour.

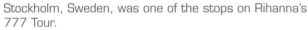

> *I'm not putting it out there as much as it is just*
> *there. You know, I can't run away from that.*
> *If I had it my way, it really would be nobody's*
> *business, but I can't escape that.*[2]

THE TERRIBLE TOUR

Rihanna's team came up with an unusual idea to promote *Unapologetic.* Rihanna rented a Boeing 777 airplane and invited 150 writers and photographers to join her on a tour of seven cities in seven days to promote her seventh album. The 777 Tour began on November 14 and ended on November 20, 2012, visiting Mexico City, Mexico; Toronto, Canada; Stockholm, Sweden; Paris, France; Berlin, Germany; London, United Kingdom; and New York City.

It was a disaster. The invited guests felt like hostages because they often weren't able to get off the plane. They went without sleep, food, or proper bathroom breaks for up to 36 hours. In addition, they had very little access to Rihanna and had to resort to begging for "just one quote."[3] The stress intensified until a riot broke out on the plane between Berlin and London. On May 6, 2013, the Fox television network aired a documentary of the tour. But some reporters said it didn't show the reality of what they lived through during the tour.

FOR PUBLIC CONSUMPTION

While she tries to keep some things personal, Rihanna has been known to make some things very public via Instagram. She has posted photos of herself partially undressed, smoking, partying in clubs, or having private moments with Brown. By posting these photos, Rihanna has seemingly encouraged the public's feeding frenzy.

Her mother, Monica, has scolded her famous daughter for revealing these moments to the world. "I'm not afraid of any person in this world, but my mother," said Rihanna. "She reeled me in about . . . pictures [my friend] put up on Instagram. She went crazy on me, I was . . . embarrassed. I felt like I got . . . whipped in front of my class at school. She humbled . . . me."[4]

RIRI'S TATTOOS

Rihanna currently has at least 19 tattoos. "I am so intrigued by tattoos. It's an entire culture, and I study it," Rihanna said.[5] Her favorite tattoo artist, Keith "Bang Bang" McCurdy, has done approximately 12 of her tattoos. After getting a new tattoo, he said, "[Rihanna] always flips out and jumps up and down like a 16-year-old girl getting her first car."[6]

Rihanna's openness on social media sites has made her the focus of both fascination and criticism.

But Rihanna continues to share tidbits with her Twitter and Instagram followers. "I Instagram everything about my life . . . to tell the truth about myself," Rihanna said. "Why [confuse things] by being dishonest?"[7] As long as fans have an interest in her private life, the media is sure to cover Rihanna's every move, especially anything she shares willingly.

||||||||||

Rihanna made a stop in Toronto, Canada, during her Diamonds World Tour.

CHAPTER 9

The Future of Rihanna

|||||||||||||||||||||||||||||||||||||||||||||||||||||||||||||||||||||

Rihanna kicked off her Diamonds World Tour in March 2013, to promote her seventh album, *Unapologetic*. The tour reflected the name of her hit single, "Diamonds," which reached Number 1 on the *Billboard* chart. The concerts opened with Rihanna kneeling on stage in a long black flowing cape, her hands clasped around a microphone as if in prayer. She sang, "Love Without

Rihanna designed her Diamonds World Tour concert to contain five segments, with different moods and themes and elaborate costumes for each one. There were scores of dancers in costumes, and the center stage revolved in a circle, while images flashed on huge screens. At one point, flames shot straight up from the stage just behind Rihanna, creating the illusion the singer was on fire.

Tragedy/Mother Mary," a song confessing her attraction to a love she knows isn't good for her: "What's love without tragedy? . . . I swear by the moment, I'm prepared to die in the moment."[1]

But Rihanna's prayerlike mood didn't last long. She removed her black cape to reveal a skimpy black and gold outfit with thigh-high black boots as she performed her boastful hip-hop song "Phresh Out the Runway." Audiences roared when she launched into her hit song "Birthday Cake," shaking her hips and striking provocative poses.

LONGING TO "STAY"

The Grammys have been significant for Rihanna throughout her career. Held in February each year, they seem to set the tone for what happens in the next year of her life. At the 2013 Grammys, Rihanna took home the award for Best Short Form Music Video for her song "We Found Love" with Calvin Harris. And her elegant and heartfelt performance of "Stay" with singer-songwriter Mikky Ekko at the 2013 Grammys was considered her best ever—and very unlike her usual friskier fare.

Ekko wrote "Stay" for Rihanna about her feelings for Brown. "'Stay' is a story about having love that close and wanting it to last forever," she said in an interview with *ELLE* magazine. "You don't want to let go of it. I would definitely say that [Brown] is the one I have that kind of relationship with."[2]

Early in 2013, Rihanna seemed confident she and Brown could make it work. But the spring of 2013 was filled with Twitter battles between Rihanna and Brown, including accusations of unfaithfulness, for the whole world to see. As of June 2013, it appeared as if their on-again off-again relationship was off again.

Rihanna gave a very emotional performance of "Stay" with Mikky Ekko at the 2013 Grammys.

OTHER PROJECTS

With all the emotional turmoil in her personal life, Rihanna remained the irreverent bad girl. She was rumored to be partying hard and arriving late to concerts and charity events during the spring and early summer of 2013.

Although her early performances during the Diamonds World Tour were initially sparkling, they seemed to turn lackluster by the summer of 2013. Fans complained about how she appeared to lip-synch some of her songs and merely swayed to the music instead of dancing and strutting with her usual energy. Some wondered if Rihanna's heart wasn't in the performances or if she was spending too much energy on other ventures.

In June 2013, Rihanna appeared in actor Seth Rogen's comedy *This Is the End*. The film starred several Hollywood celebrities playing themselves as they faced the apocalypse. Many of the celebrities died in comical ways in the film.

GIVING FOR GRANDMOTHER

Rihanna has stayed close with her family, particularly her grandmother, Clara Braithwaite, a woman she greatly respected. Before Rihanna's "Gran Gran Dolly" died of cancer in June 2012, Rihanna flew to her bedside in Barbados to spend time with her.

When Rihanna traveled to Barbados again in 2012, she donated $1.75 million to the Queen Elizabeth Hospital in Bridgetown in memory of her late grandmother. Because of her donation, worth more than $3.5 million in Barbadian dollars, the hospital was able to purchase three crucial pieces of equipment.

The hospital's radiology department was renamed the Clara Braithwaite Centre for Oncology and Nuclear Medicine in honor of Rihanna's grandmother. Of the donation, Rihanna said, "This was my way of giving back to Barbados in a form of philanthropy, by assisting the [hospital] in its continued modernization program. . . . This was all done to save lives or at least extend them."[3]

DreamWorks Animation announced in June 2012 Rihanna had signed on to lend her vocal talents as the voice of a teen girl in *Home*, an animated film about a goofy alien hiding out on Earth. *Home* was scheduled to premiere in 2014.

Rihanna has turned her love for fashion into a line of clothing, fragrances, and makeup. She designed her own collection for River Island with the assistance of the clothing company's designers. The collection incorporates cool street styles and chic, elegant looks—all the things Rihanna loves to wear.

In late 2012, the Style Network announced it was teaming up with Rihanna on *Styled to Rock*, with her as executive producer. It was a new reality series in which 12 young designers competed to create styles for some of the hottest celebrities.

COME TO BARBADOS!

Rihanna has become a tourism ambassador for Barbados. In 2010 and 2012, she was part of the Barbados Tourism Authority's promotional campaigns to attract more tourists to Barbados. In a 2013 Barbados promotional video, Rihanna was shown riding a horse on the beach, playing dominoes with locals, and frolicking in the ocean waves, while her song "Diamonds" played in the background.

Rihanna showed off her new fashion line with River Island design partner Adam Selma at London Fashion Week in February 2013.

Styled to Rock was scheduled to premiere in late 2013.

Rihanna also partnered with MAC Cosmetics to create four mini-collections of lipsticks, blush, and bronzers, with names such as RiRi Woo, RiRi Hearts, and Barbados Girl. Rihanna also developed four fragrances: "Reb'l Fleur" (2010), "Nude" (2012), "Rebelle" (2012), and "777 Nude" (2013).

LEGACY AND FUTURE

By the time she was 25 years old, Rihanna had already become the top-selling digital artist of all time. *Unapologetic* was her sixth album to reach platinum status. By June 2013, she had sold approximately 10 million albums worldwide, as well as 50 million digital downloads.

> "I will probably have a kid . . . I'll have set some things up so I don't have to tour for the rest of my life, even though I love touring. I want health and happiness in five years. I want to be healthy and happy."[5]
>
> —*RIHANNA*

One small proof of Rihanna's status and star power was the single "Walks Like Rihanna" by British boy band the Wanted. The single, released in June 2013, describes Rihanna's signature strut and a girl all the boys are drawn to: "She can't sing, she can't dance. But who cares? She walks like Rihanna!"[4]

It is too early in Rihanna's life and career to know what her legacy will be, but she has shown

Rihanna looks to continue finding success not only as a singer
but through other projects as well.

the world she is incredibly resilient, capable, and
creative. She has bright opportunities in multiple
areas of entertainment and what she does with
them is up to her. That is something her fans
already know and love about her: Rihanna strives
to be herself. Rihanna makes no apologies for
who she is, what she wants, or who she loves—no
matter what anyone thinks.

||||||||||

TIMELINE

1988
Robyn Rihanna Fenty is born on February 20 in Saint Michael Parish, Barbados.

2003
Robyn auditions in Barbados for Evan Rogers in December.

2004
Robyn and her mother fly to the United States to work on voice and record demos.

2006
Rihanna headlines in her first concert tour, Rihanna: Live in Concert, starting in July.

2006
Rihanna starts the BELIEVE Foundation, a charity to help children in need around the world.

2007
In March, Rihanna releases "Umbrella," which stays at Number 1 for several weeks.

2005	2005	2006

Robyn auditions for Jay Z and signs a record deal with Def Jam Records. She changes her stage name to Rihanna.

Rihanna's first single, "Pon de Replay," reaches Number 2 on the *Billboard* Hot 100. Her first album, *Music of the Sun*, is released in August.

Rihanna releases her second album in April, called *A Girl Like Me*.

2007	2007	2007

Rihanna releases her third album, *Good Girl Gone Bad*, on May 30.

Rihanna becomes the new face of CoverGirl cosmetics in the summer.

The Good Girl Gone Bad Tour begins in September.

TIMELINE

2007

Rihanna wins her first American Music Award (AMA) for Favorite Soul/R&B Female Artist in November.

2008

In February, Rihanna wins her first Grammy for "Umbrella," featuring Jay Z.

2008

In November, Rihanna wins two AMAs for Favorite Pop/Rock Female Artist and Favorite Soul/R&B Female Artist.

2010

The Last Girl on Earth Tour begins in April and runs until March 2011.

2010

Rihanna releases her fifth album, *Loud*, in November.

2011

In February, Rihanna wins the Grammy for Best Dance Recording for "Only Girl (in the World)" and the Brit Award for Best International Female Solo Artist.

2009	**2009**	**2010**

Rihanna is hospitalized after boyfriend Chris Brown assaults her in February.

Rihanna's fourth album, *Rated R*, is released in November.

Rihanna wins her second Grammy for "Run This Town," a collaboration with Jay Z and Kanye West.

2011	**2012**	**2013**

The Loud Tour begins in June and runs through December.

Rihanna makes her acting debut in *Battleship* in May.

The Diamonds World Tour begins in March.

GET THE SCOOP

FULL NAME

Robyn Rihanna Fenty

DATE OF BIRTH

February 20, 1988

PLACE OF BIRTH

Saint Michael Parish, Barbados

SELECTED FILMS

Battleship (2012), *This Is the End* (2013)

ALBUMS

Music of the Sun (2005), *A Girl Like Me* (2006), *Good Girl Gone Bad* (2007), *Rated R* (2009), *Loud* (2010), *Talk That Talk* (2011), *Unapologetic* (2012)

TOURS

Rihanna: Live in Concert (2006), Good Girl Gone Bad Tour (2007–2008), Last Girl on Earth Tour (2010–2011), Loud Tour (2011), 777 Tour (2012), Diamonds World Tour (2013)

SELECTED AWARDS

- Won the 2007 and the 2008 American Music Award for Favorite Soul/R&B Female Artist.

- Won the 2008 Grammy for Best Rap/Sung Collaboration for "Umbrella" with Jay Z.

- Won the 2011 Grammy for Best Dance Recording for "Only Girl (In the World)."

- Won the 2013 Grammy for Best Short Form Music Video for "We Found Love" with Calvin Harris.

PHILANTHROPY

In 2006, Rihanna started the BELIEVE Foundation, a charity committed to raising awareness about the impact of blood cancers such as leukemia. The BELIEVE Foundation also provides tangible assistance to children in need around the world.

"Robyn is the brick to my foundation. It's something I hold on to. It's everything I grew up with, my childhood, Barbados, people close to me. Everything that's familiar. People know Rihanna from my music. But if this were to all go away tomorrow, I would always look at myself as Robyn."

—*RIHANNA*

GLOSSARY

apocalypse—The total destruction of the world.

Billboard—A music chart system used by the music recording industry to measure record popularity or sales.

catharsis—The release of negative emotions, often through the creation of music or other forms of art.

chart—A weekly listing of songs or albums in order of popularity or record sales.

collaborate—To work together in order to create or produce a work, such as a song or album.

debut—A first appearance.

demo—An initial recording meant to demonstrate a musician's talent to a record producer.

felony—A serious crime usually involving harm to another person.

genre—A category of art, music, or literature characterized by a particular style, form, or content.

Grammy Award—One of several awards the National Academy of Recording Arts and Sciences presents each year to honor musical achievement.

mentor—A trusted counselor or guide.

provocative—Serving or tending to excite or stimulate.

repertoire—The entire collection of an artist's work.

satire—A story or song using ridicule or sarcasm to point out foolishness.

single—An individual song that is distributed on its own over the radio and other mediums.

studio—A room with electronic recording equipment where music, television, or film is recorded.

tempo—The speed at which a song is played. Up-tempo is fast; down-tempo is slow.

ADDITIONAL RESOURCES

SELECTED BIBLIOGRAPHY

Eells, Josh. "Rihanna, Queen of Pain: Sexting, Bad Boys, and Her Attraction to the Dark Side." *Rolling Stone*. Rolling Stone, 14 April 2011. Web. 2 July 2013.

Wilde, Jon. "Rihanna: Million Dollar Baby." *Daily Mail Online*. Daily Mail, 19 Sept. 2009. Web. 2 July 2013.

FURTHER READINGS

Govan, Chloe. *Rihanna: Rebel Flower*. London: Omnibus, 2012. Print.

Heatley, Michael, and Graham Betts. *Rihanna: Bad Girl*. London: Flame Tree, 2012. Print.

Henwood, Simon. *Rihanna*. New York: Rizzoli, 2010. Print.

WEB SITES

To learn more about Rihanna, visit ABDO Publishing Company online at **www.abdopublishing.com**. Web sites about Rihanna are featured on our Book Links page. These links are routinely monitored and updated to provide the most current information available.

PLACES TO VISIT

Barbados Tourism Authority
PO Box 242, Harbour Road, Bridgetown, Barbados
246-427-2623
http://www.visitbarbados.org
Visit this tropical paradise and Rihanna's birthplace.

Madame Tussauds Hollywood Wax Museum
6933 Hollywood Boulevard, Hollywood, CA 90028
323-798-1670
http://www.madametussauds.com
Rihanna's wax statue is on display with other celebrity wax
figures at this famous wax museum.

SOURCE NOTES

CHAPTER 1. THE POWER OF RIHANNA

1. "Rihanna-Rehab (AMA 2008)." *YouTube*. YouTube, 2 July 2009. Web. 30 May 2013.

2. "Rihanna Accepting Pop Rock Female AMAs 2008." *YouTube*. YouTube, 12 Apr. 2009. Web. 30 May 2013.

3. "Rihanna 50th GRAMMYs 2008 Acceptance Speech." *YouTube*. YouTube, 2 Aug. 2011. Web. 30 May 2013.

4. Ibid.

5. "2008 Grammy Awards Winner's Circle." *Access Hollywood*. NBC Universal, n.d. Web. 30 July 2013.

6. Rihanna (rihanna). "It's a big day in Billboard history!!!! We Rihwrite records over here!" 22 Apr. 2013, 10:13 a.m. Tweet.

7. Stella McCartney. "Rihanna." *Time*. Time, 18 Apr. 2012. Web. 10 May 2013.

8. Scott Kara. "Rihanna: Under Her Spell." *New Zealand Herald*. New Zealand Herald, 14 Mar. 2013. Web. 2 May 2013.

9. Jim Farber. "Concert Review: Rihanna Rocks the Prudential Center." *New York Daily News*. New York Daily News, 29 Apr. 2013. Web. 1 May 2013.

CHAPTER 2. ISLAND GIRL

1. Jon Wilde. "Rihanna: Million Dollar Baby." *Daily Mail Online*. Daily Mail, 19 Sept. 2009. Web. 2 July 2013.

2. Margeaux Watson. "Caribbean Queen: Rihanna." *EW.com*. Entertainment Weekly, 22 June 2007. Web. 1 July 2013.

3. Pete Samson. "Rihanna Sold Clothes in a Street Stall." *The Sun*. The Sun, 21 Jan. 2011. Web. 1 May 2013.

4. Jon Wilde. "Rihanna: Million Dollar Baby." *Daily Mail Online*. Daily Mail, 19 Sept. 2009. Web. 2 July 2013.

5. Ibid.

6. "Shontelle." *Totally Barbados*. Totally Barbados, n.d. Web. 9 May 2013.

CHAPTER 3. RISING STAR

1. Eric Danton. "Discovering Rihanna among Storrs Native Evan Rogers' Credits." *Hartford Courant*. Hartford Courant, 18 May 2012. Web. 13 May 2013.

2. "Rihanna." *People*. People, n.d. Web. 13 May 2013.

3. Margeaux Watson. "Caribbean Queen: Rihanna." *EW.com*. Entertainment Weekly, 22 June 2007. Web. 1 July 2013.

4. Eric Danton. "Discovering Rihanna among Storrs Native Evan Rogers' Credits." *Hartford Courant*. Hartford Courant, 18 May 2012. Web. 13 May 2013.

5. Jon Wilde. "Rihanna: Million Dollar Baby." *Daily Mail Online*. Daily Mail, 19 Sept. 2009. Web. 2 July 2013.

6. "Rihanna." *Biography.com*. A&E Networks Television, n.d. Web. 8 May 2013.

7. "Rihanna." *People*. People, n.d. Web. 13 May 2013.

8. Josh Eells. "Rihanna, Queen of Pain: Sexting, Bad Boys, and Her Attraction to the Dark Side." *Rolling Stone*. Rolling Stone, 14 Apr. 2011. Web. 29 Apr. 2013.

9 Ibid.

CHAPTER 4. FLYING AS RIHANNA

1. Jon Wilde. "Rihanna: Million Dollar Baby." *Daily Mail Online*. Daily Mail, 19 Sept. 2009. Web. 2 July 2013.

2 Ibid.

3. "Exclusive Interview With Rihanna." *ARTISTdirect*. ARTISTdirect, 12 May 2006. Web. 1 May 2013.

4. Ibid.

5 "Rihanna - A Girl Like Me Album Review." *Contactmusic*. Contactmusic, 2006. Web. 19 May 2013.

6. Sal Cinquemani. "Rihanna: A Girl Like Me." *Slant Magazine*. Slant Magazine, 24 Apr. 2006. Web. 20 May 2013.

CHAPTER 5. *GOOD GIRL GONE BAD*

1. Sylvia Patterson. "Singing in the Rain." *The Guardian*. Guardian News and Media, 25 Aug. 2007. Web. 19 May 2013.

2. Jon Wilde. "Rihanna: Million Dollar Baby." *Daily Mail Online*. Daily Mail, 19 Sept. 2009. Web. 2 July 2013.

3. Ibid.

4. Margeaux Watson. "Caribbean Queen: Rihanna." *EW.com*. Entertainment Weekly, 22 June 2007. Web. 1 July 2013.

5. Nekesa Mumbi Moody. "Top 10 Albums of 2004." *Associated Press*. Today, 14 Dec. 2004. Web. 1 June 2013.

6. Paul Asay. "Rihanna's a Good Girl Gone Bad." *Plugged In*. Plugged In, 2 July 2007. Web. 19 May 2013.

7. "Umbrella Star Rihanna Is Being Showered with Global Success." *Mirror Lifestyle*. Mirror Online, 29 Feb. 2008. Web. 29 May 2013.

8. "The-Dream Says Rihanna Does His Songwriting 'Justice.' *Rihanna Daily*. Rihanna Daily, 3 June 2013. Web. 31 July 2013.

9. Tamara Hardingham-Gill. "CoverGirl Rihanna Is Reinstated." *Daily Mail*. Daily Mail, 25 June 2009. Web. 1 June 2013.

10. "Rihanna's Fashion Faves." *Seventeen*. Hearst Communications, n.d. Web. 2 June 2013.

11. "The Believe Foundation - Founded by Rihanna." *BELIEVE Foundation*. BELIEVE Foundation, n.d. Web. 20 May 2013.

CHAPTER 6. DISTURBING EVENTS

1. "Rihanna and Chris Brown Get Wet in Jamaica." *People*. People, 26 Feb. 2008. Web. 1 June 2013.

2. Geoff Martz and Lauren Sher. "Rihanna Exclusive: 'He Had No Soul in His Eyes.'" *ABC News*. ABC News, 6 Nov. 2009. Web. 5 June 2013.

3. Ibid.

4. "Rihanna Wears Sunglasses in First Public Appearance Since Alleged Attack." *Star Pulse*. Star Pulse, 22 Feb. 2009. Web. 5 June 2013.

5. Geoff Martz and Lauren Sher. "Rihanna Exclusive: 'He Had No Soul in His Eyes.'" *ABC News*. ABC News, 6 Nov. 2009. Web. 5 June 2013.

6. Laurie Sandell. "Rihanna: Back on Top!" *Glamour*. Condé Nast, 3 Nov. 2009. Web. 31 July 2013.

7. Greg Kot. "Album Review: Rihanna, 'Rated R.'" *Chicago Tribune*. Chicago Tribune, 20 Nov. 2009. Web. 5 June 2013.

8. Ibid.

CHAPTER 7. *LOUD* AND PROUD

1. "Stranded (Haiti Mon Amour)." *YouTube*. YouTube, 31 Jan. 2010. Web. 1 June 2013.

2. "Rihanna Feels Strong Bond With Haitian Earthquake Victims." *Contactmusic*. Contactmusic, 25 June 2010. Web. 31 July 2013.

3. Tim Walker. "Rihanna: Out for Revenge." *The Independent*. Independent Digital News and Media, 24 Sept. 2011. Web. 1 June 2013.

4. Jonathan Van Meter. "Rihanna: Living Out Loud." *Vogue*. Condé Nast, 16 Mar. 2011. Web. 1 June 2013.

CHAPTER 8. LIFE IN THE SPOTLIGHT

1. "Rihanna Explains 'Unapologetic' Album Title and Confirms New Fragrance 'Nude.'" *Capital FM*. This Is Global, 18 Nov. 2012. Web. 10 May 2013.

2. Lewis Corner. "Rihanna Talks New Chris Brown Duet 'Nobody's Business.'" *Digital Spy*. Hearst Magazines, 9 Nov. 2012. Web. 2 May 2013.

3. Emily Zemler. "Rihanna '777' Tour Survivor Calls Documentary 'Watered-Down Propaganda.'" *Hollywood Reporter*. Hollywood Reporter, 7 May 2013. Web. 30 May 2013.

4. Derrick Bryson Taylor. "Rihanna's Mother Scolds Her over Risqué Instagrams." *Essence*. Essence, 11 Mar. 2013. Web. 18 May 2013.

5. "Tattoos." *Rihanna Daily*. Rihanna Daily, 9 Feb. 2013. Web. 1 June 2013.

6. Ibid.

7. Natalie Finn. "Rihanna Talks Chris Brown: 'Now That We're Adults, We Can Do This Right.'" *E! Online*. E! Online, 1 Mar. 2013. Web. 31 July 2013.

CHAPTER 9. THE FUTURE OF RIHANNA

1. "Love Without Tragedy/Mother Mary Lyrics." *MetroLyrics*. CBS Interactive, n.d. Web. 29 April 2013.

2. Margaret Eby. "Rihanna Says She 'Will Probably Have a Kid,' Reveals She Wants Relationship with Chris Brown to 'Last Forever.'" *New York Daily News*. New York Daily News, 2 Mar. 2013. Web. 9 June 2013.

3. "Caring Rihanna Donates $1.75m to Barbados Cancer Hospital in Honour of Her Gran Gran Dolly." *Mail Online*. Daily Mail, 24 Dec. 2012. Web. 7 June 2013.

4. Alicia Adejobi. "'She Can't Sing, She Can't Dance': The Wanted Premiere New Track 'Walks Like Rihanna'" *Entertainmentwise*. Giant Digital, 29 Apr. 2013. Web. 5 June 2013.

5. "Rihanna Baby? Pop Star Says She Wants a Kid in the Near Future." *HuffPost Celebrity*. Huffington Post, 2 Mar. 2013. Web. 5 June 2013.

INDEX

"All of the Lights," 79
American Music Awards, 7–9

Barbados, 10, 14, 17, 18, 27, 91, 92
Barbados Cadet Corps, 24–25
Battleship (film), 74–75
Berg, Peter, 74–75
"Birthday Cake," 80
Braithwaite, Clara (grandmother), 91
Braithwaite, Monica (mother), 17, 20–21, 28–29, 35, 84
"Break It Off," 41, 43
Brit Awards, 73
Brown, Chris, 59–63, 64, 67, 80, 84, 89

"Cold Case Love," 66
CoverGirl, 55

Def Jam Records, 31–32, 34, 37–38, 43, 47–48, 51–52, 71
"Diamonds," 87, 92
"Disturbia," 60
"Don't Stop the Music," 51, 53
Drake, 13, 72, 76

Ekko, Mikky, 89
Eminem, 12, 13, 76, 77

Fenty, Rajad (brother), 18
Fenty, Ronald (father), 10, 17, 19–21
Fenty, Rorrey (brother), 17

"Girl Like Me, A," 41
Girl Like Me, A (album), 40–43, 45
Good Girl Gone Bad (album), 49–53
Good Girl Gone Bad: Reloaded (album), 57, 60
Guetta, David, 81

Harris, Calvin, 89
"Hate That I Love You," 51, 53
Home (film), 92
Hope for Haiti Now, 69–70

Jay Z, 10, 13, 31–34, 38, 45, 47–48, 49, 51, 70
Jordan, Jackie, 27–28, 35

Kemp, Matt, 67
"Kisses Don't Lie," 41
Knowles, Beyoncé, 8, 24, 32, 47–48, 49, 53, 70

Layne, Shontelle, 25
Loud (album), 71–72, 77
"Love the Way You Lie," 76, 77
"Love Without Tragedy/ Mother Mary," 87–88

Music of the Sun (album), 38–41, 45

Nash, Terius, 81
Ne-Yo, 41, 45, 49, 53, 65, 81
"Nobody's Business," 81–82

"Only Girl (in the World)," 72, 73, 76

"Photographs," 66
"Pon de Replay," 31, 38–39

Rated R (album), 65–67, 72
"Rehab," 8
Reid, Antonio "L. A.," 32–34
Rihanna
    albums. *See individual album titles*
    assault, 60–65
    awards, 8–11, 39, 40, 45, 53–55, 73, 76, 79–80, 89

childhood, 17–25
criticism of, 43, 47, 67, 73–74, 77
discovery, 27–28
education, 18, 24–25, 29
fan base, 12
musical influences, 24, 49
philanthropy, 56–57, 69–70, 91
social media, 12–13, 84–85
style, 48, 55, 92
tattoos, 84
tours, 13, 41, 43, 45, 53, 56, 72, 76–77, 83, 87–88, 90–91
Rogers, Evan, 27–31, 35
"Rude Boy," 66
"Run This Town," 70
"Russian Roulette," 66

"S&M," 73
"Shut Up and Drive," 51
"SOS," 41–43
"Stay," 88–89
"Stranded (Haiti Mon Amour)," 70
"Stupid in Love," 67
Sturken, Carl, 29–31
Styled to Rock, 92–93

Talk That Talk (album), 77
This Is the End (film), 91
Timberlake, Justin, 13,
  49–50, 65

"Umbrella," 10, 51–55
Unapologetic (album),
  81–83, 87, 94
"Unfaithful," 43

"Walks Like Rihanna," 94
"We Found Love," 79, 89
West, Kanye, 70
"What's My Name?," 72, 73,
  76

ABOUT THE AUTHOR

DeAnn Herringshaw has been working as a writer, editor, and writing consultant since 1998. She especially enjoys research because she loves the challenge of learning and sharing new information and ideas. She currently lives in Minnesota.